My home

RODERICK HUNT

Pictures by Cliff Wright

Oxford University Press

1996

'This is my home,' said Snake,
with a soft hiss.

'This is what I would miss.
To slide through the scrub
and the dry yellow grass,
over sand
and land the colour of brass,
baked by the sun's kiss.'

3

'This is my home,' said old Ape, with a gruff grunt.

'In this jungle my song is sung.
Once I was strong.
Then I swung high in the trees
where ripe fruit is hung,
and clung to branches and vines,
among the insects and bees.'

5

'This is my home,' said Gull,
with a high cry.

6

'On this cliff
where the stiff winds
lift me sky high,
and the green sea sings below me,
and I drift on spread wings
under the blue sky.'

'This is my home,' said town Fox,
but she made no sound.

'I live on old land
where wild weeds have sprung.
And when night begins
I sniff for the smell
and the whiff of the bins
where old food is flung.'

'This is my home,' said Bear,
with a sure snore.

'I let winter pass –
when ice is like glass,
and bitter winds blow.
I dig deep with my paws
and long sharp claws
and make a cave in the snow.'

11

'This is my home,' said Seal,
with a short snort.

12

'In the glass-green sea
I slide into pools
and glide with the tide.
I swim below cliffs
and feed in the weed
on small fish of all sorts.'

13

'This is my home,' said Girl,
with a loud shout.

'With friends in my class
I play ball by the wall,
or race round on the grass
while long sunny days pass.

This is what I would miss –
my Ted, my soft bed, and a kiss.'

This is our home.

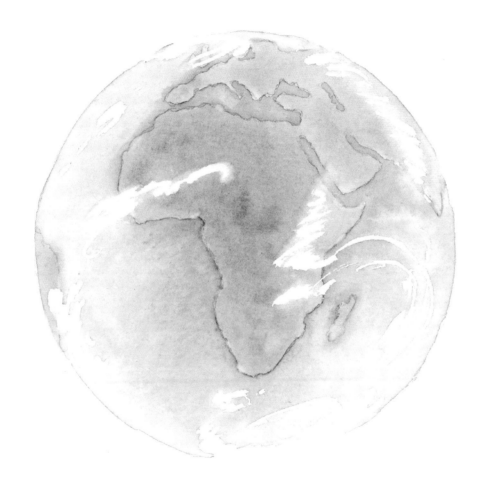